We Like Sports

by Steve Jones

I can swing at a ball.

I can help a ball over a net!

I can jump and kick fast.

I can kick a ball very far.

I can use a club now.

I can hit this ball, too!

Comprehension Check

Retell

Use an Author's Purpose Chart to describe the sports you read about.

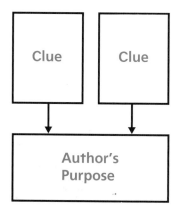

Think and Compare

1. What did the author want you to know about these sports? Describe what you can do with a ball in sports.
2. Which sport do you like best?
3. Name two team sports.